AF348466

THOUGHTS *to* INSPIRE

SHRI RAMANA MAHARSHI

SANAGE PUBLISHING HOUSE

Copyright © 2020 Sanage Publishing House LLP

All rights reserved. No part of this publication may be reproduced, distributed or transmitted in any form or by any means, including photocopying recording, or other eletronic or mechanical methods, without the prior written permission of the publisher, except in the case of brief quotations embodied in critical reviews and certain other noncommercial uses permitted by copyright law. For permission requests, write to the publisher, addressed "Attention Permissions Coordinator," at the address below.

Paperback: 978-811900772-1

Any references to historical events, real people, or real places are used fictitiously. Names, characters, and places are products of the author's imagination.

Sanage Publishing House LLP
Mumbai, India

sanagepublishing@gmail.com

Ramana Maharshi (30 December 1879 – 14 April 1950) was an Indian Hindu sage. He is widely thought of as one of the most outstanding Indian spiritual leaders of recent times. Having attained enlightenment at the age of 16, he was drawn to the holy mountain of Arunachala in southern India, and remained there for the rest of his life. Attracted by his stillness, quietness and teachings, thousands sought his guidance on issues ranging from the nature of God to daily life.

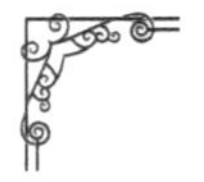

CONTENTS

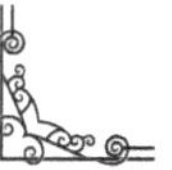

QUOTES ON SELF-REALIZATION

"Wanting to reform the world without discovering one's true self is like trying to cover the world with leather to avoid the pain of walking on stones and thorns. It is much simpler to wear shoes."

"Your own Self-realization is the greatest service you can render the world."

"All that is required to realize the Self is
to be still. What can be easier than that?"

"The real is as it is always. We are not creating anything new or achieving something which we did not have before."

"The Self cannot be found in books. You have to find it for yourself in yourself."

"The only useful purpose of the present birth is to turn within and realize the Self."

"Bliss is not added to your nature; it
is merely revealed as your true and
natural state, eternal and imperishable.
The only way to be rid of your grief is to
know and be the Self."

"The revelation or intuition arises in its own time and one must wait for it."

"Action and knowledge are not obstacles
to each other."

"We are that. The very fact that we wish for liberation shows that freedom from all bondage is our real nature."

"When we stop regarding the unreal as real, then Reality alone will remain, and we will be That."

"To do self-enquiry and be that 'I am' is the only thing to do. 'I am' is reality. I am this or that is unreal. 'I am' is truth, another name for Self."

"Self-enquiry is the one infallible means,
the only direct one, to realize the
unconditioned, absolute being that you
really are."

"A man should surrender the personal selfishness which binds him to this world. giving up the false self is the true renunciation."

SPIRITUAL MIND QUOTES

"If we regard ourselves as the doers of
action we shall also be the enjoyers of
the fruits of such action."

"There is no greater mystery than this: being reality ourselves, we seek to gain Reality."

"Solitude is a function of the mind. A man attached to desires cannot get solitude wherever he may be, whereas a detached man is always in solitude."

"One should try to gain equipoise of mind under all circumstances. That is willpower."

"The only freedom you have is to turn your mind inward and renounce activities there."

"The mind can do nothing by itself. It emerges only with the illumination and can do no action good or bad, except with the illumination."

"When he falls asleep the whole idea
vanishes; his mind is left a blank."

"It is the human mind that creates its
own difficulties and then cries for help."

"A man may be sleeping here with his body inert, and yet he may be climbing hills and falling from them in dream at the same time."

"Thoughts come and go. Feelings come and go. Find out what it is that remains."

"When we give up regarding the unreal
as real, then the reality alone will
remain and we will be that."

"In deep sleep mind is merged and not destroyed. That which merges reappears."

"You can only stop the flow of thoughts
by refusing to have any interest in it."

"The spark of spiritual knowledge (jnana) will consume all creation."

"Your true nature is that of infinite spirit. The feeling of limitation is the work of the mind."

"Calmness is the criterion of spiritual progress. Plunge the purified mind into the Heart."

"A realized one sends out waves of spiritual influence in his aura, which draw many people towards him."

"If your spiritual practice itself assumes the existence of the limitations, how can it help you to transcend them?"

"The degree of freedom from unwanted thoughts and the degree of concentration on a single thought are the measures to gauge spiritual progress."

QUOTES ON GOD

"When the wrong identification of oneself with the body ceases, the master will be found to be none other than the self."

"The Higher Power knows what to do
and how to do it. Trust it."

"Stillness is the sole requisite for the
realization of the self as god."

"God takes the form of a Guru and
appears to the devotee, teaches him the
Truth, and, moreover, purifies his mind
by association."

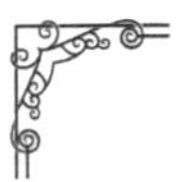

"God's will for the prescribed course of events is a good solution for the vexed question of free-will."

"All things are being carried on by the omnipotent power of a Supreme God."

"The man who prays, the prayer, and the
God to whom he prays all have reality
only as manifestations of the Self."

INSPIRATIONAL QUOTES

"Your duty is to Be, and not to be this or that."

"The ultimate truth is so simple; it
is nothing more than being in one's
natural, original state."

"The end of all wisdom is love, love, love."

"Hope for the best, expect the best, toil
for the best and everything will come
right for you in the end."

"Liberation is not anywhere outside you.
It is only within."

"Aim high, aim at the highest, and all lower aims are thereby achieved."

"Those who succeed owe their success
to perseverance."

"There is neither creation nor
destruction, neither destiny nor free
will, neither path nor achievement."

QUOTES ON HAPPINESS

"Man's search for happiness is an
unconscious search for his true Self."

"You are already that which you seek."

"Happiness is your nature. It is not wrong to desire it. What is wrong is seeking it outside when it is inside."

"If one's mind has peace, the whole
world will appear peaceful."

"Transforming yourself is a means of
giving light to the whole world."

“The solution to your problem is to see
who has it.”

QUOTES ON CONSCIOUSNESS

"Everyone knows 'I am!' No one can
deny his own being."

"Instead of indulging in mere speculation, devote yourself here and now to the search for the Truth that is ever within you."

"Mind is consciousness which has put
on limitations."

"In truth, you are spirit. The body has been projected by the mind, which itself originates from Spirit."

"Turn your vision inward and the whole
world will be full of supreme spirit."

"There is neither Past nor Future. There
is only the Present."

"But some of these rules and discipline
are good for beginners."

"No one succeeds without effort."

"All these viewpoints are only to suit the
capacity of the learner. The absolute can
be only one."

"The ultimate truth is so simple; it is nothing more than being in one's natural, original state."

"There is no Truth. There is only the
truth within each moment."

QUOTES ON EGO

"The mind turned inwards is the Self;
turned outwards, it becomes the ego
and all the world."

"If the ego does not rise, the Self alone
exists and there is no second."

"If ego rises, all will rise. If the ego
merges, all will merge. The more we are
humble, the better it is for us."

"The thought 'I' is the first thought of the mind; that is egoity. It is from that whence egoity originates that breath also originates."

"All unhappiness is due to the ego. With it comes all your trouble. If you would deny the ego and scorch it by ignoring it you would be free."

"Reality is simply the loss of ego.
Destroy the ego by seeking its identity."

"There must be a subject to know the good and evil. That subject is the ego."

QUOTES ON SILENCE

"When there are thoughts, it is distraction: when there are no thoughts, it is meditation."

"Silence is most powerful. Speech is always less powerful than silence."

"Just before waking up from sleep, there
is a very brief state, free from thought.
That should be made permanent."

"Silence is truth. Silence is bliss. Silence is peace. And hence Silence is the Self."

"Meditation helps concentration of
the mind. Then the mind is free from
thoughts and is in the meditated form."

MOST FAMOUS QUOTES

"All knowledge will have to be finally given up to experience the truth."

"There is no doubt that the end of the paths of devotion and knowledge is one and the same."

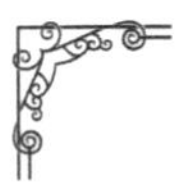

"If the light of the sun is invisible to the owl it is only the fault of that bird and not of the sun."

"You are awareness. Awareness is
another name for you."

"Mukti or liberation is our nature. It is
another name for us."

"The state free from thoughts is the only
real state."

"The Eternal is not born, nor does it die."

"Let what comes come, let what goes go.
Why do you worry?"

"I am in the heart of all beings and am
their beginning, middle and end."

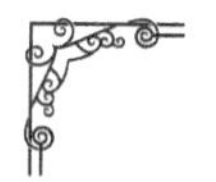

'WHO AM I' QUOTES

"When the world which is what-is-seen has been removed, there will be realization of the Self which is the seer."

"When the mind, which is the cause
of all cognition's and of all actions,
becomes quiescent, the world will
disappear."

"That which rises as 'I' in this body is
the mind. If one inquires as to where in
the body the thought 'I' rises first, one
would discover that it rises in the heart."

"It is after the appearance of the first
personal pronoun that the second
and third personal pronouns appear;
without the first personal pronoun there
will not be the second and third."

"Till the time of death, the mind keeps breath in the body; and when the body dies the mind takes the breath along with it."

"It is by virtue of the mere presence of God that the souls governed by the three (cosmic) functions or the fivefold divine activity perform their actions and then rest, in accordance with their respective karmas."

"God has no resolve; no karma attaches
itself to Him."

"One can know oneself only with one's
own eye of knowledge, and not with
somebody else's."

"In dream the mind takes on another body. In both waking and dream states thoughts. names and forms occur simultaneously."

"The process of enquiry of course, is not an easy one. As one enquires 'Who am I?', other thoughts will arise."

"Remaining quiet is what is called wisdom-insight. To remain quiet is to resolve the mind in the Self."

"Not seeking what is other than the Self
is detachment or desire lessness; not
leaving the Self is wisdom."

"Correcting oneself is correcting the
whole world."

LIST OF TITLES WITH ISBN NO.

ISBN	TITLE
9788194914129	1984
9789390575220	1984 & Animal Farm (2In1)
9789390575572	1984 & Animal Farm (2In1): The International Best-Selling Classics
9789390575848	35 Sonnets
9789390575329	A Clergyman's Daughter
9789390575923	A Study In Scarlet
9789390896097	A Tale Of Two Cities
9789390896837	Abide in Christ
9789390896202	Abraham Lincoln
9789390896912	Absolute Surrender
9789390896608	African American Classic Collection
9789390575305	Aldous Huxley: The Collected Works
9789390896141	An Autobiography of M. K. Gandhi
9789390575886	Animal Farm
9789390575619	Animal Farm & The Great Gatsby (2In1)
9789390575626	Animal Farm & We
9789390896158	Anna Karenina
9789390575534	Antic Hay
9789390896165	Antony & Cleopatra
9789390896172	As I Lay Dying
9789390896226	As You like it
9789390575671	At Your Command
9789390575350	Awakened Imagination
9789390575114	Be What You Wish
9789390896233	Believe In yourself
9789390896998	Best of Charles Darwin: The Origin of Species & Autobiography
9789390896684	Best Of Horror : Dracula And Frankenstein
9789390575503	Best Of Mark Twain (The Adventures of Tom Sawyer AND The Adventures of Huckleberry Finn)
9789390896769	Black History Collection
9789390575756	Brave New World, Animal Farm & 1984 (3in1)

9789390896240	Brother Karamzov
9789390575053	Bulleh Shah Poetry
9789390575725	Burmese Days
9789390896257	Bushido
9789390896066	Can't Hurt Me
9788194914112	Chanakya Neeti: With The Complete Sutras
9789390896042	Crime and Punishment
9789390575527	Crome Yellow
9789390575046	Down and Out in Paris and London
9789390896844	Dracula
9789390575442	Emersons Essays: The Complete First & Second Series (Self-Reliance & Other Essays)
9789390575749	Emma
9789390575817	Essential Tozer Collection - The Pursuit of God & The Purpose of Man
9789390896578	Fascism What It Is and How to Fight It
9789390575688	Feeling is the Secret
9789390575190	Five Lessons
9789390575954	Frankenstein
9789390575237	Franz Kafka: Collected Works
9789390575282	Franz Kafka: Short Stories
9789390575060	George Orwell Collected Works
9789390575077	George Orwell Essays
9789390575213	George Orwell Poems
9788194914150	Greatest Poetry Ever Written Vol 1
9788194914143	Greatest Poetry Ever Written Vol 1
9789390896301	Gulliver's Travel
9789390575961	Gunaho Ka Devta
9789390575893	H. P. Lovecraft Selected Stories Vol 1
9789390575978	H. P. Lovecraft Selected Stories Vol 2
9789390896059	Hamlet
9789390575022	His Last Bow: Some Reminiscences of Sherlock Holmes
9789390896134	History of Western Philosophy
9789390575121	Homage To Catalonia

9789390896219	How to develop self-confidence and Improve public Speaking
9789390896295	How to enjoy your life and your Job
9789390575633	How to own your own mind
9789390896318	How to read Human Nature
9789390896325	How to sell your way through the life
9789390896370	How to use the laws of mind
9789390896387	How to use the power of prayer
9789390896028	How to win friends & Influence People
9788194824176	How To Win Friends and Influence People
9789390896103	Humility The Beauty of Holiness
9789390896653	Imperialism the Highest Stage of Capitalism
9789390575084	In Our Time
9789390575169	In Our Time & Three Stories and Ten poems
9789390575145	James Allen: The Collected Works
9789390896189	Jesus Himself
9789390575480	Jo's Boys
9789390896394	Julius Caesar
9789390575404	Keep the Aspidistra Flying
9789390896400	Kidnapped
9789390896424	King Lear
9789390575824	Lady Susan
9789390896455	Law of Success
9789390896264	Lincoln The Unknown
9789390575565	Little Men
9789390575640	Little Women
9788194914174	Lost Horizon
9789390896462	Macbeth
9789390896929	Man Eaters of Kumaon
9789390896523	Man The Dwelling Place of God
9789390896349	Man The Dwelling Place of God
9789390575909	Mansfield Park
9788194914136	Manto Ki 25 Sarvshreshth Kahaniya
9789390896509	Marxism, Anarchism, Communism
9789390575664	Mathematical Principles of Natural Philosophy

9788194914198	Meditations
9789390575800	Mein Kampf
9789390575794	Memory How To Develop, Train, And Use It
9789390896486	Mind Power
9789390896585	Money
9789390575039	Mortal Coils
9789390575770	My Life and Work
9789390896035	Narrative of the Life of Frederick Douglass
9789390575152	Neville Goddard: The Collected Works
9789390575985	Northanger Abbey
9789390896530	Notes From Underground
9789390896547	Oliver Twist
9789390575459	On War
9789390575541	One, None and a Hundred Thousand
9789390896554	Othelo
9789390575435	Out Of This World
9789390575015	Persuasion
9789390575510	Prayer The Art Of Believing
9789390575091	Pride and Prejudice
9789390896561	Psychic Perception
9789390575381	Rabindranath Tagore - 5 Best Short Stories Vol 2
9789390575367	Rabindranath Tagore - Short Stories (Masters Collections Including The Childs Return)
9789390575374	Rabindranath Tagore 5 Best Short Stories Vol 1 (Including The Childs Return
9789390896622	Romeo & Juliet
9789390896127	Sanatana Dharma
9789390575596	Seedtime & Harvest
9789390896639	Selected Stories of Guy De Maupassant
9789390575206	Self-Reliance & Other Essays
9789390575176	Sense and Sensibility
9789390575299	Shyamchi Aai
9789390896738	Socialism Utopian and Scientific
9789390896646	Success Through a Positive Mental Attitude
9789390575428	The Adventures of Huckleberry Finn

9789390575183	The Adventures of Sherlock Holmes
9789390575343	The Adventures of Tom Sawyer
9789390896691	The Alchemy Of Happiness
9789390575862	The Art Of Public Speaking
9789390896288	The Autobiography Of Charles Darwin
9788194914181	The Best of Franz Kafka: The Metamorphosis & The Trial
9789390575008	The Call Of Cthulhu and Other Weird Tales
9789390575107	The Case-Book of Sherlock Holmes
9789390896110	The Castle Of Otranto
9789390896745	The Communist Manifesto
9789390575589	The Complete Fiction of H. P. Lovecraft
9789390575497	The Complete Works of Florence Scovel Shinn
9789390896820	The Conquest of Breard
9789390896813	The Diary of a Young Girl
9789390896332	The Diary of a Young Girl The Definitive Edition of the Worlds Most Famous Diary
9789390575701	The Great Gatsby, Animal Farm & 1984 (3In1)
9789390575312	The Greatest Works Of George Orwell (5 Books) Including 1984 & Non-Fiction
9789390575992	The Hound of Baskervilles
9789390896707	The Idiot
9789390896714	The Invisible Man
9789390575657	The Knowledge of the holy
9789390575558	The Law & the Promise
9789390896721	The Law Of Attraction
9789390896776	The Leader in you
9789390896363	The Life of Christ
9789390896196	The Man-Eating Leopard of Rudraprayag
9789390896783	The Master Key to Riches
9789390575268	The Memoirs Of Sherlock Holmes
9789390896479	The Midsummer Night's Dream
9789390575466	The Mill On The Floss
9789390896790	The Miracles of your mind
9789390896660	The Mutual Aid A Factor in Evolution
9789390896448	The Origin of Species

9789390896905	The Peter Kropotkin Anthology The Conquest of Bread & Mutual Aid A Factor of Evolution
9789390896806	The Picture of Dorian Gray
9789390896271	The Picture of Dorian Gray
9789390575275	The Power Of Awareness
9789390896356	The Power of Concentration
9788194824169	The Power of Positive Thinking
9789390575411	The Power of the Spoken Word
9788194914105	The Power Of Your Subconscious Mind
9789390896899	The Power of Your Subconscious Mind
9789390896417	The Principles of Communism
9789390575787	The Psychology Of Mans Possible Evolution
9789390896615	The Psychology of Salesmanship
9789390575732	The Pursuit of God
9789390575398	The Pursuit of Happiness
9789390896851	The Quick and Easy Way to effective Speaking
9789390575947	The Return Of Sherlock Holmes
9789390575138	The Road To Wigan Pier
9789390896981	The Root of the Righteous
9789390575855	The Science Of Being Well
9788194914167	The Science Of Getting Rich, The Science Of Being Great & The Science Of Being Well (3In1)
9789390896011	The Screwtape Letters
9789390896073	The Screwtape Letters
9789390575336	The Secret Door to Success
9789390575695	The Secret Of Imagining
9789390896868	The Secret Of Success
9789390896431	The Seven Last Words
9789390575930	The Sign of the Four
9789390896004	The Sonnets
9789390896516	The Souls of Black Folk
9789390896875	The Sound and The Fury
9789390575244	The State and Revolution
9789390896882	The Story of My Life
9789390896936	The Story Of Oriental Philosophy

9789390896752	The Strange Case of Dr. Jekyll and Mr. Hyde
9789390896943	The Tempest
9789390575916	The Valley Of Fear
9789390575879	The Wind in the willows
9789390896080	The Wind in the willows
9789390575763	Their eyes were watching gofd
9789390575831	Three Stories
9789390896950	Twelfth Night
9789390896592	Twelve Years a Slave
9789390896677	Up from Slavery
9789390896974	Value Price and Profit
9789390896967	Wake Up and Live
9789390896493	With Christ in the School of Prayer
9789390575602	Your Faith is Your Fortune
9789390575473	Your Infinite Power To Be Rich
9789390575251	Your Word is Your Wand
9789390575718	Youth
9789391316099	A Christmas Carol
9789391316105	A Doll's House
9789391316501	A Passage to India
9789391316709	A Portrait of the Artist as a Young Man
9789391316112	A Tale of Two Cities
9789391316747	A Tear and a Smile
9789391316167	Agnes Gray
9789391316174	Alice's Adventures in Wonderland
9789391316136	Anandamath
9789391316181	Anne Of Green Gables
9789391316754	Anthem
9789391316198	Around The World in 80 Days
9789391316013	As A Man Thinketh
9789391316242	Autobiography of a Yogi
9789391316266	Beyond Good and Evil
9789391316761	Bleak House
9789391316778	Chitra, a Play in One Act
9789391316310	David Copperfield

9789391316075	Demian
9789391316785	Dubliners
9789391316051	Favourite Tales from the Arabian Nights
9789391316235	Gitanjali
9789391316068	Gravity
9789391316150	Great Speeches of Abraham Lincoln
9789391316662	Guerilla Warfare
9789391316839	Kim
9789391316822	Mother
9789391316211	My Childhood
9789391316846	Nationalism
9789391316327	Oliver Twist
9789391316853	Pygmalion
9789391316334	Relativity: The Special and the General Theory
9789391316389	Scientific Healing Affirmation
9789391316341	Sons and Lovers
9789391316587	Tales from India
9789391316372	Tess of The D'Urbervilles
9789391316396	The Awakening and Selected Stories
9789391316402	The Bhagvad Gita
9789391316303	The Book of Enoch
9789391316228	The Canterville Ghost
9789391316907	The Dynamic Laws of Prosperity
9789391316006	The Great Gatsby
9789391316860	The Hungry Stones and Other Stories
9789391316433	The Idiot
9789391316440	The Importance of Being Earnest
9789391316297	The Light of Asia
9789391316914	The Madman His Parables and Poems
9789391316457	The Odyssey
9789391316921	The Picture of Dorian Gray
9789391316464	The Prince
9789391316938	The Prophet
9789391316945	The Republic
9789391316518	The Scarlet Letter

9789391316143	The Seven Laws of Teaching
9789391316525	The Story of My Experiments with Truth
9789391316532	The Tales of the Mother Goose
9789391316549	The Thirty Nine Steps
9789391316594	The Time Machine
9789391316600	The Turn of the Screw
9789391316983	The Upanishads
9789391316617	The Yellow Wallpaper
9789391316426	The Yoga Sutras of Patanjali
9789391316990	Ulysses
9789391316624	Utopia
9789391316679	Vanity Fair
9789391316020	What Is To Be Done
9789391316686	Within A Budding Grove
9789391316693	Women in Love

www.ingramcontent.com/pod-product-compliance
Lightning Source LLC
LaVergne TN
LVHW040019070726
842759LV00026B/527